# Tea With Our Monsters

## Poems from
## a Mental Health Journey

*Aimee Larson*

# An Odd Introduction

Monsters do not make appointments. They do not call to say, "I'll be checking myself into your mind on Tuesday. I plan on staying for a few days. I may invite a few friends over, so you may hear some partying."

Mental illness sometimes comes with warning and I feel the darkness creeping in. Then, sometimes I have hours or days where things seem perfect, then I wake up feeling like happiness is a distant memory. I wish there was an On / Off switch. I wish there was a magical tea or wine offering I could give my monsters to convince them to come back another day, or not at all. But there is no magic potion. There are good days and there are bad days and none of them can be scheduled, planned, or moved around.

This collection of poems talks about my struggles with mental illness and mental health. I write about the monsters of anxiety, depression, bipolar, and others. I was initially going to categorize these poems and put them in order: one section for mental illness and one for mental health. However, I decided against it. With Mental illness there is no schedule order, and I wanted this collection to reflect that.

Lack of order does not mean lack of hope. Even if the monsters come without warning, we can learn to fight them and learn how to cope with them through the dark times and the better times.

I want my readers to know you are not alone. Sometimes our minds can be real jerks and place our thoughts on a Ferris wheel and then refuse to stop the ride. There are going to be days where giving up seems easier. There are going to be days where life feels like it is going backwards. But we can take a step back, face our monsters, and say, "I see that you have returned. I will not let you keep me down."

There will be brighter days, despite what our minds may say.

There will be moments of laughter, despite the tears that may come.

Here you stand, ready to take on the world.

Here you stand, ready to find your voice to continue on.

Look at you and how far you have come.

This is your journey and your path.

You are not alone.

You got this.

Welcome the world of *Tea With Our Monsters*

# Contents

# PART 1

# Searching for your Voice

Remember to breathe, sweet child.
Your trembling heart shows that you are alive.
Never forget your soul
For you are not your diagnosis.
Show yourself,
You can find the light in the darkness.
Never forget the shadows that may follow,
But do not let them take over.
You are not alone, warrior.
No matter how much pain,
May come knocking inside.
You will find your voice.

# Will To Live

Treasures can be found throughout life,
With only enough energy,
To breathe and fight another day.
Wanting to grasp onto the gems,
And hold them close to the heart.
Yet simply the thought of searching.
Leaves me feeling numb and wanting more.
Wishing to be more,
Other than the person,
That I woke up as of today.
I have no energy,
other than fighting for the will to live.
Against my worst enemy,
Me.

# Wizard Lost and Found

Searching for the wizard,
Throughout the darkest days.
Blinded throughout the storm.
Attempting to find the energy,
To verbalize the words
Of the darkness that comes in waves.

Searching to find a way,
To fight against the monsters
After staying silent for so long.
Almost forgetting what a truthful smile
Felt like despite better days.

Lost and found,
A wizard came forth.
A long road ahead,
Full of therapy and medication.
The monsters may continue to rave on,
But not without a fight.

# Time To Speak

Stitch up the corners of your lips.
Your daily performance is about to begin.
Cannot forget the foundation,
Not this time, nor ever again.
Act the part in many of your roles.
Take a bow at the end of it all.
Can you feel the applause of those
That should not matter?
For slowly,
We can see that you are breaking
In society standards,
Of blissful ignorance.
If only you could see
Your mask is slowly suffocating
As you continue to drain
Your inner resources
Without speaking a word
I wish you could break your silence.

# Creativity

The act of creativity,
Is a constant struggle,
Between what should
And should not exist.
Creativity allows the mind,
To express and find the words,
For the meaning of life's madness.
While allowing the beauty to be found
Treasuring the lost little gems within.

# Tea with Monsters

Despite a heavy weight of doubt.
I am still here, breathing.
Sitting in a room with my inner monsters
As we drink tea and they lick their lips.
Expecting and voicing my future downfall.
Despite the setbacks that may come.
I am still here, alive.
Ready to take on the unwelcomed,
And fight day by day
With a newfound strength and open arms.
I am here and I am very much alive.

# Symbol Etched In Stone

Into the darkness I venture into,
Wherein the symbol of a world, I fade.
Such a beauty in the life I built as stone.
A symbol engraved within.
Left alone and surrounded by lies.
For fear is a powerful tool
And the enemy keeps me content
In the world of stone I know best.

# Daytime Storms

Both dreadful and ensuring.
Things that feed the seven thunders,
Throughout the daytime storms.
Continue to break my trance
Of thoughts throughout the day.
Fear and assurance of being alive
Despite the long-term numbness.

# Inner Battle

In a kingdom full of battles,
My mind is in revolt.
The enemies are at the gate
The monsters have gotten through.
My mind strays away
From the anxious thoughts
Dismisses depression's attack.
Only to continue to fall
Into the same steps of injury
Without consideration of defense
Letting the old wounds reopen
In fear of failure, of trying something new.
Yet insanity by definition
Is trying the same thing repeatedly
Expecting a different result
Waiting for a mental change
Without a fight.

# An Eternal Love

Underneath the scattered stars,
Focusing on the moonlight.
A love is found,
In the darkest of times.
A love well deserved
Despite all the inner wars going within.

# Just a Rabbit

Eyes staring at my body,
Awkward movements apparent.
Through the pack of wolves, I go.

Anticipation of mental attacks,
Holding back the tears
As the perceived judgement arises.

Fear clawing inside my soul.
As tears beg to be free.
Among the eyes, that stare.

Through a fake smile,
I continue in silence
Among the wolves I seek.

# Self–Care

A sense of relief,
Through the days,
Where life feels normal.
Sadness will come again.
Regardless of my objections.
For now, though,
I will enjoy a mental break.
Resting peacefully as needed,
And preparing for the wars that lie ahead.

# A Mental Castle

Within the grounds of the kingdom,
Delicate flowers bloom.
Regrowing through the recovery process.
Within the castle's grounds.
My mind still wanders within the darkness
Captivated by familiarity.
Straying towards the safe trap
Within the castle of protection
Craving for the solitude of habit
Fearing the failure within the maintenance
Of the soil that lives within.

# Carving False Truths

Monsters carving themselves within,
Leaving hidden scars.
A fake plastered smile for the crowd.
Not even a whisper,
To speak the truth
Of the monsters that
Reside within.
No rent to pay,
Other than the damage
Left behind.

# Feast For The Monsters

A dream,
Threatened by reality
Of anxious thoughts.

Flashes of sound
As the heart beats faster
In anticipation of threat.

The thunder rolls in,
Lights flickering, alternating
Between darkness and light.

The monsters feast
Upon the hopeful dream
Ignoring the pleas for them to leave.

Saliva dripping down their chins
Expecting such flavor
As I lose grip on reality.

The monsters ripping the flesh off the bones,
Years of built up strength
Naked on their plates.

Time spent on a dream
Only to feed the monsters
That lives within.

Left only with the bones
That I alone must rebuild and strengthen
For the next time around.

# Tell Me More

Nighttime dreaming in hell.
Flames making their way to the surface,
Rage at the unknown
Uncertain on how to gain control.
What is to come?
What is next?
In this odd, forsaken world.

Mind playing tricks.
Easy to pull the trigger
Tears streaming down my face,
Uncertain what to feel anymore.
Should I stay numb?
Tell me, what is next?
In this game, my mind likes to play.

Sit across from me,
As I speak of my inner demons.
Sadness and Madness intertwining within.
Uncertain if I should even be here.
Will you understand?
Will you judge the flavor of my soul?
In this life, I am losing grip on reality.

# The End

The sweet whisper,
Of death closing into my flesh.
The memories of life.
Outside these walls
As I glance out,
The closed window.
I wonder,
If love will remember
After my body withers away.

# An Inner Hell

Rising from the depths,
Of her inner hell.
Carrying with her,
A once silenced story.
Within the pages bound,
Held her voice and her truth.
Ready for the world
With her newfound voice.

# A Grave of Memories

Deep into that darkness touring,
Back into memories of what once was.
Throwing ghosts against the storms
Of a voiceless night.

Through the grave, I walk,
Reliving the best memories.
When your voice was close.
Now alone in the silence.
Attempting to find my inner light.

# Work In Progress

My passion is a rhythmic item,
A cultural concept in idleness.
Working through the blank canvas.
As I continue to push,
Through the inner boundaries.

The walls are breaking down,
Freedom finally within proximity.
A life with potential setbacks,
Fighting for a work in progress,
For an art piece worth living.

# Writing Warrior

Continue to write,
Throw the beast
Into the neck of the woods

Continue to watch
Don't listen
The depressed blistering words

Continue the war
Through the splinters
Buried deep within

Continue to want
Your own voice
To fight with the wounded

Continue on, warrior
You are part
Of this ugly and beautiful world.

# The Writer's Soul

Fighting for words
Forcing the pen
Ignoring toxic thoughts

Words whisper aloud
Onto the blank pages
Quieting the inner hell

Remembering my heaven
Where wine opens the gates
Into the light of creativity

Fear holds no power
When I am in control
Of my writing bliss.

# Tired of Communicating

When the words run dry,
The silence surrounds us
We do not force communication.
In stillness,
We can be together.
Without the distractions of words.
Acknowledging each other's tiredness,
For the world around me.
Loving each other's presence,
While allowing one another to recharge,
For a better tomorrow.

# Tell A Story

Born under the same sky,
Once the cries sound,
A story begins.
A story from birth
The battles of upbringing
Understanding the world around
Through many senses.
Many lives intertwined,
Perhaps not a permanent knot.
But an intercross of greetings
And learning throughout.
Many lives were touched.
Many lessons were found.
Throughout a strange life.
A story continues
To read in between the lines.
Continuing a story,
A breath of life.
Your story does not end here.

# The Power of Words

Language can be Earth shattering,
Upon building and breaking a soul.
Words can be left scattering.
Leaving a toll,
On the human mind.

# An Artful Life

Painted images trapped on the canvas,
Shades of blue
Throughout the once white fabric.
Attempting to find the right stroke,
To express to the outer world.
The battle within
The words unexpressed
To create a sense of unspoken familiarity
With the acrylic paint.

# A Game of Life

Life is strange
Constantly losing the sense of time.
While attempting to fit into today's society.
Life understood backwards,
Yet attempting to stay present.
Without losing yourself
In the comparison game.

A story unfinished
Waiting to be written in the words
Of the life you have experienced.
Life lived in a forward direction.

# A Garden Grows

A mind once full of destruction,
Filled with fear and despair
For events that would never come.

A mind once filled with fighting
Still filled with the remnants of past battles
Now a garden.

A gentle reminder into reality,
A truth of the value of one's life
Despite the old consuming lies.

Now, a will to question those lies
Within the garden
A constant reminder to keep going.

# Succulent Plant

Watching past mistakes
Of the inexperienced succulent.
Over watered and left drowning,
Within my captivity.

Recording recent memories,
Breathing into the present
Attempting a balance
Between insanity and staying sane.

# Dehydrated Flower

You were a beautiful, unique flower
So strong through the deepest storms
Now your petals are being plucked
By those you call your friends.
You are letting your life wilt
To be part of the crowd
You continue to dehydrate yourself
From the pure joy you deserve
Will it still be there
When the nights get colder
And there is no warmth
In the darkness?

# The Garden

Days turned into weeks
As the flowers wither
In the familiar garden
That once was safe haven
Now only death alums.

Time lost value
In a dying garden
Where dreams were no longer
Worth the upkeep
In this state of mind.

Forever a dying garden
I weep in silence
As death looms closer
For her sweet kiss.

# Life

Living in a delicate and temporary world
Full of life
Waiting for the perfect time to bloom
Despite the many nights,
Alone under the moon.

Living for the stars
That surrounds the night
A gentle reminder
That beauty can bloom
In darkness.

# The Forest

Mind lost,
In the never-ending forest
Alone in every direction
Returning to nothing
I continue to let myself down
Losing everything
I continue forth
In the blinding forest
That never seems to end
Uncertain of where it leads
In hopes
To gain a better sense of self
In a future unknown
Fighting for the light
In the darkest hour
That seems through the trees.

# Lotus Flower

The flower slowly blooms,
After submerging itself underwater
Throughout the night.
Re-blooming for another day,
Its petals open one by one.
Taking in the world around,
As its roots latch into the mud.

The flower continues to flourish.
Taking everything day by day.
Becoming a beautiful gift.
Despite the murky waters.

# Dandelions

Messy emotions scattered throughout
Dispersing seeds over long distances
Waiting to grow
And pop up later, when they are not wanted.

The struggle to see the beauty in the weeds.

# Poisoned Life

I continue to poison my soul
Perhaps out of habit or fear
Dehydrating myself with comparison
Among the sunflowers
That surrounds the same soil I live in.
Who am I?
To feel the need to dream,
Of a world
Where do all flowers bloom the same?
I may not know my answer,
in this world, that I am a  part of
I will continue on
in my own unique way
Acknowledging when I harm my soul
Push through for a better me
A better version of me in a future worth living.

# Someday is Today My Love

Day after day,
I wish my fingers could forever trace,
Upon your warm body.
Forever, I crave to embrace your essence.

Day after day,
I wonder if I could face you,
And tell you the truth.
Forever, I wish to be a part of your world.

Day after day,
I fear the unknown,
To tell you of the broken.
Forever, I hope to be your love.

Day after day,
Today will be that day.
That I speak my truth.
Forever, I embrace your strangeness.
And hope that you embrace mine.

# Allowing Love

Whisper the peaceful notes on the bars again
Of a smooth melody filled with dreams
Mark my heart with a sense of hope.
Want me for me,
Versus the guilt, you may feel
If you see the truth in the darkness.

Our lives are intertwining as one,
As your heart senses,
When my mind is amiss.

Be part of my world,
That will bring upon wrinkles
As we hold hands through it all.

# Last Piece

Words at the tip of my tongue
Wishing for answers to come easy
To place a piece of the puzzle
Into your life
I wish I had the right words
But I don't know what to say.
All I can do is provide my presence
And hope for the best
Through your dark times.

# My Strange Love

A strange love
You are my type of weird
In a world that is full of oddness
Despite my scars
I find you holding me
Without another thought on my flaws
Wanting to know both the light
And the darkness
That captivates my soul.

# Learning to Love Again

Imagine all you could achieve
With self-love
The feeling of righteousness
To one's emotions
More than a mental wish
On a shooting star
Growing through multiple seasons
Accepting opposites
Day by day
One breath at a time,
Knowing repeatedly you are loved
And have a right to live.

# Love In The Broken

I will continue to endure,
The love we share.
As we embrace
In each other's broken pieces.
Understanding each other's darkness.
I never thought,
This type of love could exist.
Not for my heart to have.
Yet here you stand,
Nervously revealing,
Your own cracks and bruises,
That life has handed you.
I can't help but smile,
As our inner beasts intertwine,
A familiar and yet unfamiliar scent
Of love found at last.

# Love in the Darkness

When darkness captivates my soul,
And silence surrounds us
You hold me gently
Ensuring me the monster is lying.
Gentle smiles pass between us.
As your presence
Brings comfort in the darkest hours.

# My Heart, My Brain, My Soul

My heart,
Thrown into the rain
Shivering in the cold,
The thoughts come.

Too much of a hassle
For the world in front of me.
Too much of an annoyance
For my heart to stay warm.

My brain,
Tossed in the grinder
Blades spinning
Slaughtered into pieces.

Too many thoughts,
At all the what-if moments
That make no logical sense.
Too much for my mind to stay sane.

My soul
Wishing for a life
Where the flowers can grow
in a well-tended garden.

Too much damage,
To ignore my heart and mind.
But I continue

Looking for ways to grow my flowers
Attempting to dismiss my own very thoughts.

# Moving On

My actions were never enough
No matter what I did
You filled me up with thoughts
That left my mind spiraling
Questioning every movement
In fear of your anger.
Feeling the need to walk
Around the broken glass you left.

A light shined through,
I saw my worth
I saw my value
And it did not include you.
I pushed, you begged.
I kept my feet grounded
It was time to let go
Of what I thought we had.

# PART II

# Dear Anxiety

Dear Anxiety
Lying becomes more natural
Now that your roots
Seem to intertwine into me
Weaving in and out of my heart
Waiting for moments
To throb and sink your thorns
Into the muscle of my core.

Fear of speaking of your existence.
Punisher and tormentor
As you throw in thoughts
Of negative magnitude
Resulting in overthinking
Every choice I make.

You are the toxic voice in my head
Telling me I am not good enough
I lie awake,
Wishing I could have enough courage
To speak my truth.
Of your existence.
Without fear of negative consequences.

You lie to keep me awake
Leaving me tossing and turning
Wanting only silence
Instead of the chatter within

My passage and my truth
Despite the inner battle with myself
I have a right to exist.

# Clarity Notice

There are moments,
That overlaps with one another.
A loss of memory
Forgetfulness of the present.

Loss of senses
Amplifying the noises around.
Confusion and irritation
Scrambling for a logical reason,
behind my brain attacking itself.
No reason other than
Everything is the enemy
As the pathways flare up,
Fight, flight, or freeze.
At a moment's notice,
A calm situation
Can trigger a mental fight.

# Invincible

Throughout my body,
My heartbeat races
As it takes a hold of me once more.
This feeling of excitement,
A dangerous feeling
Of feeling invincible.
How can something that feels so good?
Am I wrong?

The universe is my oyster.
As I collect the pearls
With no regard to the dangers
Of the intense waves that follow.
I continue to burn myself out,
Like a falling star.
Crashing into melancholy.

Left alone with my own worst enemy.
Plans made and canceled,
A different mode of existence,
Yet knowingly the same soul.
Of this meat suit, I call my body.

# Social Interactions

Words drift away
As I ponder where to begin.
In a conversation full of possibilities
Attempting to find the right words
In a puzzle full of potential outcomes.

Heart races faster and faster
Panic slithering inside
Wrapping hold to a solid weight
Upon my chest.
A present moment in an internal war.

# The Familiar

A lonely place to be,
With no real rhyme or reason
Perhaps with time,
I will get better.

Time came,
The feelings stayed.
Perhaps with success,
This emotion will go away.

Success came,
In waves
Perhaps feeling normal is not for me.
And this familiar feeling will stay forever.

My anxiety came
And continued to stir
Beaten around in a bowl.
Waiting for a taste in reality.

My emotions came
Giving me every reason to worry.
Every breath
is up for judgment.

# Talk to Me

Covered with broken promises.
Waiting for the truth to come out.
My mind's playing games,
Making up the truths
For the reasons
you speak differently now.

Is it me? Or is there something else going on?
Whispers clawing into my mind,
My fault, my fault.
Uncertain of what I did wrong.
Tell me you are alright,
And it's not me that is to blame.

# The Upcoming Storm

The clouds in the sky
Come roaring in
As the voices get louder
Changes are coming
As the thunder replies
Prepare for the upcoming storms
Life will become unsteady.
As the rain falls.
The sun will shine through the clouds
In the darkest point of the storm
Here you stand
One of life's greatest warriors
Through the depths of pain and joy
You will get through this
But not alone.

# Silence

On that day, my soul grew silent.
Back into the memories, muting.
Staying quiet within the downpour.
Waiting for the emotions,
To cause such numbness.
Shivering to become resilient
Only to dive further into the depths,
Of a mind lost in a forever loop.

# Sleepless Nights

I laid engaged and waiting
I crave the standstill, searching for sleep
That standby, standby shivering.
Wanting to count the sheep.
Only my mind cluttering,
Leaving me only to weep.

# Social Induced Anxiety

Alone in the crowd
As people continue to walk by
Footsteps echoing
As the heart panics
Finding it difficult to breathe
Without any reason
Other than anxiety
Taking a hold once more
Unknown fear sitting upon my chest.
No logical reason.
For the existence of a threat.
other than my mind,
Fearing for no escape
In an open space
With no barriers
To hold back my departure.

# My Worst Enemy

Whispers in a silent room
No use running
Slowed steps echo.
All the faceless
Staring into my soul.
Judging my heartbeat,
In the crowd of familiar faces.

# Crowded Anxiety

A need for space
After many conversations
And energy spent in the crowd
Craving for solitude
Despite the heart shared
With the familiar.
Power draining low
As the heart beats faster
Looking for an exit
A space to breathe
and gather thoughts
With no one witnessing the panic
Creeping outside of my mask
A need for space,
To recharge and learn to breathe again.

# Stigma

I cannot help but notice the man
Continuing down into the spiral of darkness.
Gently, he tries to blend into the crowd.
Attempting to leave without fearing
Wishing for the wounds to no longer be visible.

How I mourned the compassion.
Yet fear for the status of his own mind.
The stigma surrounding mental health
And the definition of strength.

A world we continue to live in,
Down, down, and down into the darkness
Promoting to show strength through silence.
Instead of fighting through voice.

# Railway track

A railway track that leads in the same direction,
Despite the surroundings of many.
Different viewpoints and life experiences
Among this same path.
A track leading to choices
Of those that have felt alone
Under the midnight stars.
Little has changed in the environment,
Yet everything is all the same.

# Mental Soundtrack

Turn up the music,
Continue to drown out the thoughts.
With each thought that passes through,
The sense of threat increases
There is no threat
Hold the lyrics close to home,
When you are at a loss for words.
Wanting only to be alone within the crowd.
Turn up the song,
That shakes upon your soul
When you are feeling lost and uncertain.
Get lost in the music.

# Mental Inbox

Messages in my mind,
Icons blaring notifications
Leaving me blind
And alone to life's hallucinations.

Ignore the junk mail,
That wants to take control,
of my derailment.
Control the messages
that want to take over.

# Mental Cage

A prisoner bound in chains
Waiting for the will to escape
Energy quickly draining
As the thoughts continue forth
A never-ending cycle
Upon what I thought to be deserved
In a self-made cage
Where the monsters dance
In life's performance
And I find myself the star.

# Dear Depression

Another day has arrived
And I am greeted by you once more.
In an underwater prison,
Attempting to remember
What the sun looks like.
Another mind fog
Lost in my head
Confused
Disoriented.
For no reason
Except you.

I wish to be enjoying life,
But I don't even remember
What that even feels like anymore.
Loss of interest
Loss of the ability to even recharge.
I lay here awake
Trying to come up with the will
To do the easiest of tasks.
Even the simplest of tasks
Require getting out of bed
And facing the day.
The energy to find a smile,
As you keep me in your prison.

# The Key

Standing still
As the world keeps moving.
Frozen in place
Attempting to break free
From my own inner prison
Find the rusty key
To move past the bars
Of self-containment.

# Lost In Thoughts

Lost in deep thoughts
Daydreaming of past wishes.
When passion fed the fire
That kept life interesting.
Left only with an empty shell
Of what once was.
Dreaming to find purpose,
In an empty room
That I found myself once again.

# Reflection

Reflection, a tormentor of my dreams.
Pondering and ridiculing
The lack of action and motivation

"Exercise More!"
Without consideration for the lack
Of energy, motivation, or power
To move through the day
With a heavy burden of survival.

"Eat better!"
Without consideration for the emptiness
That exists within
Or the feeling of under or overeating.
To fill an emptiness,
That suffocates to the very core.

Reflection.
Attempting to find a way.
To love the person on the other side
Of the mirror.

# A Moment In Waiting

I waited and waited,
For the moments to return.
The moments where I smiled
For real.

I waited and waited,
For the color to return.
To the world in darkness.
Alone again.

I waited and waited,
For the sun to rise,
And bring a smile
Once again I lost myself.

# Chatter in the skull

Lights out
As the voices dance.
Twisting my senses
Against reality.
More! The beast yells.

Power to the beasts
That lives within.
Failure written on my wrists.
Another day once more.
No more!

Lights on,
The beast screams.
Pushing the blade further
Fighting against my mind.
As I continue to breathe again.

# Too Many Emotions

Emotions so strong,
Sometimes the desire
For wanting numbness
Is stronger,
Than we can ever imagine.
Despite our inner prayers,
The emotions continue,
To throb uncontrollably.
Until there is nothing left
But an empty shell of what once was.

# Self Medication

Put down the bottle,
You are not fooling anyone.
In this world's throttle.
Depression waits for no one.

The poison upon your lips.
Makes the heart grow weaker.
Upon the anxious trips,
A self-medicated filled beaker.

Continuing to feed the beast,
Then much rather stay silent.
In a mental illness feast.
Instead of life's antidepressant.

# Society's Mirror

Staring into the mirror
Practicing smiling for the crowd
Effortless and almost natural
Society continues to label
Those who struggle inside
Smile for the people
Fake it till you make it
They say
When will they be right?

# Stand Still In Mental Time

Standing still in time
Lost in the echo
Of my wreckage.

Screaming in the white room
With only my voice bouncing off the walls
in response.

Tears streaming down,
Nails digging into the skin
To ensure the reality of time,
Accurate to my heartbeat.

Gone are the days,
Of truthful smiles
Left only with a label
To the stars of my disorder.

# I Am Enough

I am enough.
Regardless of what I may say
Later today or down the road.
I am worth it,
Despite what the outside world may say.
I will continue to luminate,
Into the darkness
And throughout the lighter days.
The demons may come,
For my past, present and future self.
I am enough,
As I am now.

# Imperfection

Thoughts breaking the silence
A constant loop of inner obsession
Fear of outer appearance
Waiting for the apparent dissection
Of the constant interference
From society's selection
In a world wanting acceptance
for labeling imperfection.

# Kintsugi

Waiting to break
into a million pieces,
Living in constant fear
To shatter once more.
Staying silent,
As the screams get louder within.

Finding self-love gold
Repairing piece by piece,
As cracks continue to grow
With every drop bled
Every cracked shard
I will continue to learn for next time.

Repair is part of a journey
Rather than hiding the cracks
My brokenness pieced together by strength
I continue to live another day
Broken
Deserving.

# Pieces

Little pieces of happiness
Throughout the day
Waiting to be admired
In the storm
Take a moment to breathe
To stay present
While working to quiet the mind
Even throughout the strangest of days,
Cherish those moments
Where smiling seems natural.

# Wood Wick Candle

Crackling in the darkness,
A light burning within.
With the scent of life,
Flickering but waiting
Until the morning light.

Clenching the lighter,
In case the fire suffocates.
Letting the fire dance
Through the silent night.
Keeping vigil
Fighting for the light.

# The Reminder of Moments

There are days,
Where my head feels too heavy
To look up into the sky.

There are days,
Where hope feels lost.
Without a reason.

There are days,
Where the very thought of another day,
Is almost too much to bear.

There are many moments,
Where you remind me,
The reason I continue to push through.

# We Are Not Alone

Sadness weighing heavily
Digging deeper within
Feeling the desperation to give up
Under the weight of it all
Feeding myself with lies,
Filled with untruths of our value.
Echoing into an endless loop,
Replaying the same tune repeatedly.

Working on a newfound voice,
To break free from this repetition
of the toxic thoughts within.
Knowing I am not alone
Despite the manipulative lies
A warrior
Deserving the beauty
Found scattered throughout.

# Strange Music

Lean in the moment
Snap out of chaotic reprise
Listen, closely
For the intermission
Upon the darkest hour
For a gentle melody
Will play upon your soul
The soundtrack will continue.

# New Experiences

There is a world beyond my window
Outside of the safe place
I created for myself alone.
Assuming others may not understand.
Perhaps someday,
Will become today.
Where I let others into this room,
And allow myself to experience
Without internal fear and judgement.

# Night Terrors

Screaming throughout the night
Locked within a nightmare
Only to wake up
With hardly any recollection
Of the nightmares
But left with a panicked heart
Attempting to catch your breath
As those that laid next to you.
Lied awake to make sure you were safe.
Through your internal battle.
That left you with no memory
Of the events that kept you stuck within.

# Coffee for Life

Voices screaming inside my head,
Doubtful intentions of waiting
Waiting for the answers in the empty cup.
Left only with the taste of the coffee.
Upon my dry lips.

Wishful thoughts,
Left with everything unanswered.
If only coffee led to life's answers.
Of what route to walk upon next.

As the routes of possibilities
Blare inside my very own soul.
Which direction to choose?
If only life choices were simple,
As simple as choosing between creamers.

A flavor for life,
An uncertain path of what's coming.
Continue forth
And drink upon uncertainty,
In this odd world, we call life.

# Coffee and a Scoop of Madness

Awake
After pointless sleep
All the overthinking
Leaving visible darkness
Under the eyes
Full of emptiness.
Lost in the deepest of thoughts,
Falling into the same routine.
Waiting for the coffee to be made,
Only to cover up the exhaust
Of every day's life in a mind of madness.
Taking a few sips,
If only the monsters would listen,
And take this coffee
As an offering for a silent mind.

# Ready or Not

Trauma placed inside of individual jars.
Left to rest on the highest shelf.
Out of sight and out of mind.

As time goes by,
Additional jars added,
With the dust continuing to collect.

A body-worn down,
A soul tired from holding back.
Pretending the trauma
Never existed.

The shelves creak,
Under the unbearable weight.
From the collection of jars.
Waiting and pleading to break.

# Priceless Diamonds

Priceless diamonds,
Streaming down my face.
Lost in the echo of the cries
Through my soul that escapes,

No witnesses for the truth.
For the show must go on.
Smile for the faceless crowd.
That feeds my soul.

Keep letting me down,
To the ground, I belong.
Stuck in my head.
That suffocates my well–being.

# Bird In The Sky

I am just a bird
That flew too far
From a broken cage.
Yet I continue to fly,

Despite my broken past.

Continue to breathe,

Continue to live in the sky,

As I struggle towards my dreams,

For a better life in the clouds.

# Relapse Road

My heart is the lonely relapse
Back into my memories, reclaiming
Somewhat louder than the taps,
That starts amplifying.
Old wounds infected within captivity.
Waiting time after time,
To continue through the grime.

Another round of trials,
Supervised medication under control.
A worthwhile fight for more miles.

# Dog Reminders

My dog
Searches in the dark for my scent
She stares into the silhouette
Of my outer shell,
Despite the tears,
She continues
Greeting me with licks
And nudges for attention
All she sees is a light inside me
Placing her head on my chest
Reminding me,
My heart continues to beat
Regardless of the emptiness,
That I continue to feel
I am still alive
And so is she.

# An Internal Stumble

Stumbling through the darkness,
Trying to find the light
Silent throughout
The internal screams
That followed past the night.
Stay silent, my mind speaks.
Fearing the very thoughts,
That poison with false truths.
My own internal fight,
No one would understand.
Nor attempt to acknowledge,
The pain that comes
Even on the normal days.

# Better Days

The beast enters once more.

After so many good days,

The creature carries words

Meant to weigh me down.

Failure and disgrace,

A useless soul wandering around.

Attempting to push me backwards.

Only this time,

I have better armor

Towards a better self-image.

I am a warrior, ready to fight.

Acknowledging the monsters

I continue forth.

Despite the creatures words,

That continues to play.

You are not alone,

Not now and not ever.

# Music Box

Inside a broken heart,
There is a song
Ready to be played once more.
A melody full of life.
Ready to be heard again.
Another soul yet to be found.
That may hold the key
To the music box within.

# Carry Onward

Listen closely, for the wind is howling,

The thunder rolls in louder each time.
Ready to take down the sails,

The ones you built by hand.

Sail into the storm,

Ready the life vest in case

The storm is too much this time around.

Carry onward through the waves.

With better knowledge that there will be light

At the end of the storm.

# A Cats Demeanor

Kneading his paws back and forth,
Into my chest.
As though attempting
A ritual for the beasts within.
His purrs grow louder,
As the tears continue
To make their way down my face.
His eyes staring into my soul.
Perhaps with judgment,
Or demanding me to move
To feed him once more.
Cats are strange creatures.
For this though,
His presence
I am grateful.

# Change

The rain is coming,
I can feel it in my bones.
Joints crackle,
As the anticipation
Of lightning dances in the sky.
No reason,
Other than the changing season,
Waiting for the rain to show itself.
So, I can see the beauty of a rainbow
At the end of it all.

# Construction Zone

Searching for a home,
Outside of my own.
Only to bear witness,
A power lost and found within.
Between both mind and body,
A place to build and feel whole again.

# Resurge

A flickering light,

Burning within.
Waiting to recharge

For a better tomorrow

After darkness had almost won.

Leaving a wounded core.

That life had chewed and spat out.

Only to gain better access

To life's never-ending battle to live.

# Phoenix

Deep into that darkness, chatting
Eagerly I looked for the ember
Back into my memories, scorching.
Wanting to remember
A life worth admiring.
Through the ashes anew.

# Rising from Ashes

Walking through fire,
And rising from the ashes,
Wearing nothing but a smile.
After gaining a sense of calm,
From speaking out loud,
Of the monsters' torment within.
He finally continues forth,
With an army gained,
After speaking his truth.
Of the relatable war within.
Ready to fight again.
Only this time
Not alone.

# About the Author

Aimee Larson knows what it's like to struggle with mental illness. She's spent her life battling her demons and resting up for the next fight. In spite of what she's been through, she also strives to light, the way out of the darkness for others, and her soul-baring poetry is designed for just that—offering a glimpse into her very real pain as a way to help others know they're not alone and find the courage to keep going no matter how tough things get. When she's not writing, Aimee enjoys reading everything she can get her hands-on, playing with her pets—a fun-loving puppy and two cats as different as night and day though they both love naps—and having a beer or glass of wine, depending on the day, her mood, and maybe even the tides of the moon because who knows? Her goal is to remind other people that while mental illnesses bring challenges, there is also beauty. She strives to help others, to be the kind of person she needs on her worst days, and to shine a stark light on the harsh reality of living with mental monsters.

# Other Books

**The Awkward Armadillo: A Mental Health Memoir**

This fun, heartfelt, and sometimes sorrowful account of growing up with anxiety, depression, and social anxiety is a journey that might reveal secrets about ourselves. The author's humor and randomness bring light to her darkest struggles in a way that's so human it resonates as you read her words.

Available on paperback and ebook

https://amz.run/4ahN

Printed in Great Britain
by Amazon